5 Book In 1

Enter the world of Blockchain, DEFI, The MetaVerse, NFTs

The Ultimate Beginners Guide to CryptoCurrency and the new world of Finance

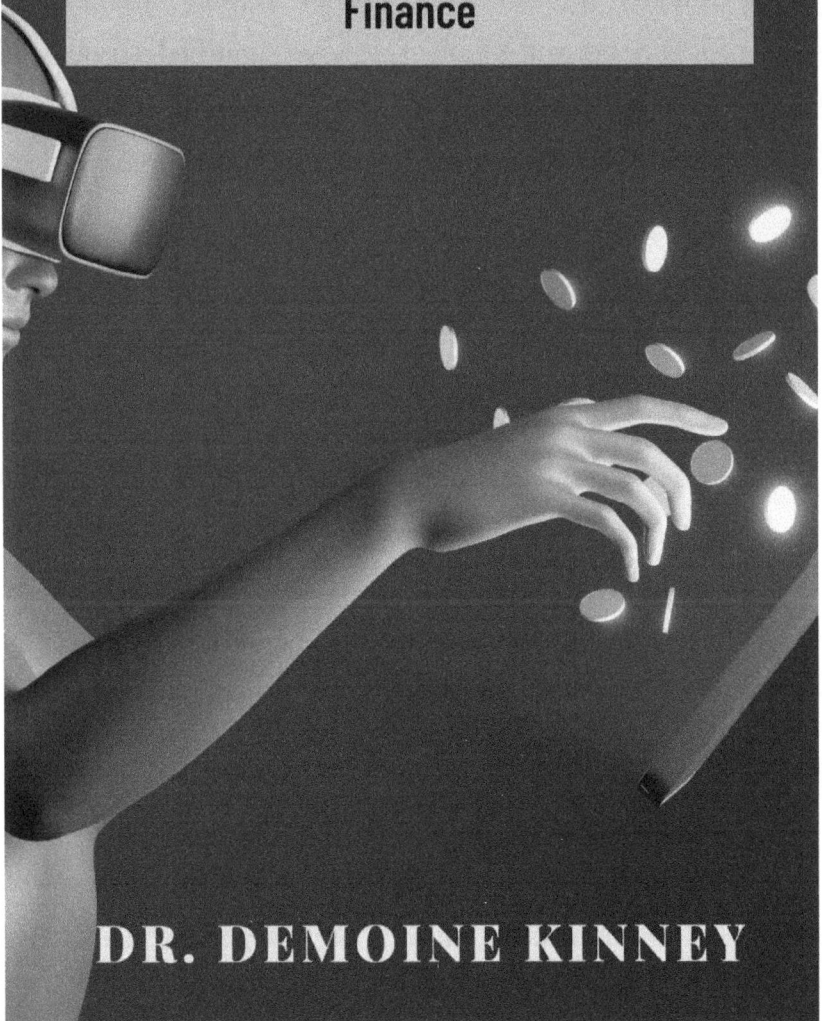

DR. DEMOINE KINNEY

policies, processes, or directions contained within is the solitary and utter responsibility of the recipient reader. Under no circumstances will any legal responsibility or blame be held against the publisher for any reparation, damages, or monetary loss due to the information herein, either directly or indirectly.

Respective authors own all copyrights not held by the publisher.

The information herein is offered for informational purposes solely, and is universal as so. The presentation of the information is without contract or any type of guarantee assurance.

The trademarks that are used are without any consent, and the publication of the trademark is without permission or backing by the trademark owner. All trademarks and brands within this book are for clarifying purposes only and are the owned by the owners themselves, not affiliated with this document.

ISBN: 978-1-953760-14-2

Table of Contents

CRYPTOCURRENCY IS THE NEW MONEY

Introduction

In 2008, someone named Satoshi Nakamoto changed the way money is transferred when he published a document that laid the foundations for paying with bitcoin, the first cryptocurrency, creating a decentralized payment network in which neither banks nor governments have a place.

Nakamoto, whose identity is not known with certainty - whether a person or a group - determined that bitcoin would be an instrument to transfer money completely managed by users, based on a peer-to-peer network or network between equals.

He did so by devising a technology that allows users to make direct exchanges with excellent security: the blockchain or chain of blocks. Conscious or not of his proposal, Nakamoto revolutionized the way of making payments.

WHAT IS CRYPTOCURRENCY

Cryptocurrencies are digital currencies, a type of currency that can be used to purchase goods and services just like any other currency but only exists in the virtual world. Unlike the physical ones, the cryptocurrency does not depend on the intervention of a centralized body to regulate its operation.

A cryptocurrency uses cryptography to provide a secure payment system. These encryption techniques serve to regulate the generation of monetary units and verify the transfer of funds. The cryptocurrency needs neither a bank nor a center or other institution that controls !. And that is one of the reasons for its great success.

The cryptocurrency universe glossary

Here are some definitions of the cryptocurrency

11

universe;

Ethereum: It is the best-known cryptocurrency after Bitcoin and consists of a public, open-source distributed network based on blockchain. It offers the development of decentralized applications and the network itself that works as an operating system for the execution of smart contracts.

Blockchain: Sometimes translated as "chain of blocks," it corresponds to the technology consisting of an encrypted, decentralized database, and distributed in user networks that store transactions and record them in data packages.

Mining: In the context of crypto-technology, this computing process consists of carrying out a series of calculations to validate transactions and thereby permanently record the information in the blocks on the blockchain network. By this process, miners receive an incentive in the form of new cryptocurrencies.

Hold: The English "hold" refers to the most fundamental investment strategy of all, buying a cryptocurrency and keeping it in the long term, waiting for a capital gain. Back in 2013, a user of the Bitcoin talk forum made a typo and entered "HODL," and since then, in crypto-economic jargon, this investment strategy has been known.

Token: It is the digital representation of an asset or service and is used as a recognized monetary unit in a specific ecosystem. There are several types of tokens, but more than 80% use the Ethereum network for their operation and offer from the equivalent value of a real asset (security token) to allow access to a series of services offered by a project (utility token).

Airdrop: Consists of the free distribution of cryptocurrencies to users or investors who meet a series of requirements, generally to publicize and disseminate a project.

Fiat: Also known as fiat money, it is any conventional form of money issued by a government, such as the Euro, Dollar, or Yen, and is based on the collective belief that this form of money has a value determined by society.

CBDC: Corresponds to Central Bank Digital Currency, or what is the same, digital currency issued by the central bank of a territory or country.

Wallet: Also known as a purse, or wallet, it is the place where you store cryptocurrencies. There are mainly cold wallets, which remain not connected to the internet and hot wallets that are always connected to the network.

DAO: It is the "Decentralized Autonomous Organization," and it refers to a form of government of organisms that, thanks to a series of smart contracts, allows executing various processes based on certain conditions without the need for human intervention.

Pool: Referred to as a "mining pool," it is a combination of several computer equipments that constitutes a network of miners to add computing power or "hash rate" and thus generate greater rewards that are then distributed among the pool members. It is a collective way of mining cryptocurrencies, and there are public and private ones.

NFT: From English Non-Fungible Tokens. This type of cryptocurrency corresponds to a token that is backed by the value of anything, from an image to a real asset such as a car or a house. NFTs differ from fungible tokens like bitcoin in that each token is unique.

Stake: The concept refers to a form of passive investment by which an amount of currency is blocked during a specific period to get additional units of that same currency. For example, the Ethereum coin offers an annual reward for "staking" of around 7% per year.

Farm: Corresponds to the platforms that allow us to obtain units of a new currency from the blocking of another cryptocurrency. For example, for blocking 100 units of currency A, five units of currency B are received each week.

DeFi: Decentralized Finance from English corresponds to decentralized finance. Financial services platforms allow the exchange of currencies and banking products directly between users and anonymously, without the control or support of a centralized entity. This allows from lending money to buying and selling assets in a disintermediated way, without financial institutions.

Parachain: They are blockchain networks that work in a satellite way and complement a leading blockchain network. For example, the Polkadot project offers parachain spaces for other networks to connect and communicate with each other.

WHAT ARE THE CHARACTERISTICS OF A CRYPTOCURRENCY?

There are infinite cryptocurrencies, but they all have some characteristics in common. These characteristics are the following:

- Cryptocurrencies are cryptographic; this means that they use encryption techniques to make both collections and payments completely safe.

- Cryptocurrencies are decentralized; this means that they do not need to be controlled by any institution.

- There is no possibility of counterfeiting or duplication of cryptocurrencies since all of them have a cryptographic system that protects users.

- Cryptocurrency transactions are irreversible; once the payment is made, there is no possibility of canceling it.

- Another of the main characteristics of cryptocurrencies is their possibility of exchange;

cryptocurrencies can be exchanged with other currencies.

- Cryptocurrencies are private; they have the privacy of use, so it is not necessary to reveal your identity when doing business.

All these characteristics are what make cryptocurrencies a sector to which many people dedicate themselves and want to dedicate themselves.

What is its value?

The market determines the value of cryptocurrencies. More than 2 trillion dollars has been invested in Bitcoin and other cryptocurrencies, probably hoping that investors will be willing to pay more for them.

One could argue that this is all a ruse to make money appear out of thin air. Each bitcoin began as a payment to a person for performing the cryptographic work on a computer that was required to record transactions on the blockchain (an activity called "mining"). However, their worth is determined by what people are willing to pay for them, which is determined by where people expect the price to go in the future.

Bitcoin's supply is confined at a level that ensures scarcity; there will never be more than 21 million bitcoins, although the world's population is currently at 7.9 billion people and growing. The greater the demand for crypto, the higher the price will rise.

Is it, in fact, a coin?

Cryptocurrencies as a medium of exchange leave a lot of room for improvement. For starters, only a few businesses accept them as payment.

A few technology companies, a couple of sports franchises, a handful of retailers, and restaurants worldwide are among the places where you can spend bitcoins. Alternatives exist, such as Purse, which allows you to exchange them for Amazon gift cards. Still, the need for such services highlights how ineffective cryptocurrency is as a dollar bill substitute right now.

Moreover, Bitcoin has not maintained its short-term value, an important characteristic of any currency. The value of the US dollar fluctuates in relation to other currencies, and its purchasing power breaks down over time due to inflation. However, it does not increase by 33% in a week, as Bitcoin did in the first week of

October 2021, nor does it lose nearly a quarter of its value in a week, as Bitcoin did in mid-May. Bitcoin prices are 30 times more volatile than the dollar, euro, or yuan, according to a 2017 study.

On top of that, you'll have to pay fees for your cryptocurrency or other blockchain transactions. These fees are typically a small percentage of the transaction's value, far less than what merchants pay to credit card processors. However, you may have to pay a higher fee if you want your transaction to be processed quickly. Otherwise, you may have to wait for hours or even days.

Why would anyone use Bitcoin or similar mechanics as a medium of exchange because of the volatile prices and other drawbacks? Perhaps because cryptocurrencies, like cash, can be spent anonymously but from afar. That could explain why digital currencies are used to pay for ransomware and illicit purchases on the dark web.

Stable coins, a type of token whose value is tied to the dollar or another non-crypto asset, are available for those who want to use their cyber currencies as currency. Tether is the most well-known of them; its creators claim that each Tether token is backed by one dollar in cash and other reserves, and its price has remained at or near one dollar for much of its history.

How do you get started on this?

The majority of cryptocurrencies are available for purchase by anyone. All you need is a way to send your order to the blockchain for the currency you're working with.

The simplest way is to use a cryptocurrency exchange, such as Binance or Coinbase. In the world of cryptocurrencies, these are akin to a shopping mall, providing access to a wide range of them. These websites will typically offer a digital wallet that resembles a checking account but is secured by a personal cryptographic key rather than a PIN. You put money or digital currencies into the wallet, and it finances your purchases, keeps track of your inventory, and saves digital receipts that show what you've bought and sold.

A "custodial" wallet is stored in the cloud and managed by a third party who can help you recover your password. One disadvantage is that it relies on centralized servers that can be hacked, as BitMart was last months, resulting in crypto losses of $ 150 million or more. Such losses may be protected by insurance, as appears to be the case with BitMart. This isn't always the case, though.

If you're concerned about such a risk, you can use your exchange to transfer your holdings to a "non-custodial" wallet that you control. It could be a computer or phone application, such as MetaMask's, or a specialized high-security USB drive (known as a "hardware wallet"). In either case, you are the only one who has access to it, and if you forget your password, you will lose your cryptocurrency.

THE 5 CRYPTOCURRENCIES THAT YOU HAVE TO LOOK AT IN 2022
Ether (ETH)

Ether is the cryptocurrency of Ethereum, the smart contract network created by Russian-Canadian programmer Vitalik Buterin.

Investors see a great prospect in the Ether cryptocurrency because the Ethereum technology is so promising - financial services are hosted there, and millions of transactions happen. For this reason, experts trust it and consider it a technological platform with high long-term projection.

This year, the Ethereum smart contract network is expected to launch a series of updates and enhancements to eventually scale to Ethereum's layer two, which promises more incredible speed, more decentralization, and low fees.

According to various analyzes from Tradingview, the digital currency Ether entered a short-term bearish scenario and is an opportunity to accumulate digital assets.

In the medium term, the crypto is expected to hit $5,000 and rise to $7,000.

Binance Coin (BNB)

The cryptocurrency has been trading under the acronym "BNB" since 2011, and today it is trading at $ 460. It's a digital currency that was launched by Binance, a popular cryptocurrency exchange, only 11 days after it began operating on a global scale.

On May 10, 2021, the crypto had reached an all-time high of $ 686, and since then, it has been down 32%. But this drop does not discourage any investor. According to the Tradingview platform, the cryptocurrency reaches $1,000 long-term.

Polygon (MATIC)

"MATIC" is a cryptocurrency based on Polygon, an Ethereum smart contract protocol that allows 65,536 transactions per second.

The goal of this crypto project was to simplify the scalability and instant transactions of Ethereum smart contracts.

This year, the digital currency reached an all-time high of US $ 2.92, and due to the bear cycle, its price fell 26%. Still, Tradingview investors say the price is "going to skyrocket" to $ 4, which is a gain of more than 30%.

Bitcoin (BTC)

Historically, the cryptocurrency Bitcoin has delivered astronomical returns to its investors. In 2010, it was trading at $0.003, and today it is around $43,000, which translates into a total profit of 1,433,333,233%.

In this context, the digital currency is expected to gain positive this year and reach a new all-time high above $69,000.

Avalanche (AVAX)

This project aims to compete with the Ethereum smart contract network. Developers can use Avalanche to create and develop decentralized applications such as investment protocols.

In addition, Avalanche promises interoperability between different blockchains, and in the future, several blockchains may be connected.

In other words, this blockchain allows asset transfers between the Ethereum blockchain and the Avalanche blockchain since it interconnects both networks.

Today, the cryptocurrency AVAX is trading at $93, and experts expect it to exceed $200. In percentage, this rise would translate into a gain of 115%.

BLOCKCHAIN

Blockchain - Concept, and what it is

As with many other fashionable things, the term Blockchain has been heard lately, sometimes referring to electronic cryptocurrencies and confidently stamping signatures on electronic documents. What does it consist of? The Blockchain (English: "chain of blocks") is a distributed database. Each item contains a timestamp and a link to a preceding document, making it theoretically impossible to edit once sealed. As a result of its high security, dependability, and verifiability, Blockchain is utilized in this type of application, which requires high reliability to avoid counterfeits. Time stamping the transaction (called a transaction in Blockchain slang) allows blockchains to store information that interests us in carrying out a quick follow-up for some reason. An example of this would be a contract that must be renegotiated annually and therefore varies once every twelve months.

What Is a Blockchain?

A blockchain is a decentralized data set divided between PC network hubs. A blockchain goes about as a data set, putting away data in a mechanical design. Blockchains are notable for their primary job in keeping a solid and decentralized record of exchanges in digital money frameworks like Bitcoin. The blockchain's curiosity is that it guarantees the devotion and security of an information record while additionally creating trust without the prerequisite for a confided-in outsider. The structure of the data on a blockchain differs from a traditional database. A blockchain organizes data into groupings called blocks, each containing data collection. Blocks have specific storage capabilities, and when they're full, they're closed and linked to the preceding block, producing a data chain known as the blockchain. It's a digital log of duplicated transactions spread across the blockchain's whole network of computers. Each square in the chain contains various exchanges, and each time another exchange happens on the blockchain. Distributed Ledger Technology (DLT) is a decentralized database administered by multiple people. Blockchain is a conveyed record innovation where trades are recorded utilizing a hash, a changeless cryptographic mark.

How does blockchain work?

The blockchain works through a distributed ledger called Distributed Ledger Technology — DLT. In this record are blocks of data in which there are digital signatures called a hash. In turn, the hash is a cryptographic biometric print. In this way, for each new block of data, a new hash linked to the previous block's hash is created for each new transaction.

The hash is potent because it is virtually tamper-proof. The blockchain, or data chain, must be broken for the data block to be broken. This is only possible by cracking a series of hash — remembering that they are all interconnected. Finally, the blockchain hash is recorded in the ledger, which is the name received by the data block ledger.

This operating logic does the work of those who seek to violate a blockchain very difficult. It is necessary to break the sequence of all blocks successively. Finally, any intermediary is unnecessary since the reliability of the transactions is guaranteed by the network members themselves. A blockchain network is essentially a database that enables the reading and writing of new records. All of the documents kept there are connected using clever mathematics. Therefore, it is difficult to include anything inconsistent with the rest of the papers.

Components of a Blockchain Network

❖ Blocks

Blocks are the foundation of a blockchain in the literal sense. Blocks feature portions designated to save data for future transactions and contain records of previous transactions. A block represents the past and future. A chain connects the different blocks of a blockchain network. When the last block's hash code is solved, the new block takes its place. A block on a blockchain network comprises hash codes, the Merkle tree's root hash, and a nonce. Miners seek to drive change in a blockchain network by solving complex hash codes. New blocks can only be added when the regulations have been decoded.

❖ Chain

A blockchain network's blocks are linked to one another. A chain of blocks is made up of multiple blocks that have been connected.

❖ Node

Blockchains are massive, storing millions of records. The machines that hold this enormous volume of data are known as nodes. Nodes are computers, laptops, and significant servers. A blockchain network's nodes are all linked together. A blockchain network's history is stored on nodes. Full nodes are similar to school attendance registers in that they maintain track of every transaction, such as which blocks are being added and which blocks are being replaced. After verifying the signatures and validating the details, nodes double-check the hash code answer and add a new block to the blockchain network. Nodes might be online or offline at the same time. Nodes also check the legitimacy of the union of transactions.

❖ Master Node

Master nodes are used in selective blockchain networks. Normal nodes are less capable than master nodes. They are in a constant activity state (24 hours a day, seven days a week). In a blockchain network, master nodes support voting events and anticipate other events. These nodes use more memory than conventional nodes, and their primary goal is to keep the blocks in balance. The addition of new blocks to the blockchain network is not the responsibility of master nodes. They make it easier for additional modifications to take place within a network. Master nodes can be found in Bitcoin, Ethereum, and Dash, among other cryptocurrencies. They are large servers that do a plethora of activities and prevent authentication.

Types Of Blockchains

Currently, there are different types of blockchain, each with its unique capabilities and characteristics that adapt to different needs. These types of blockchain are public, private, hybrid, or federated.

1. **Public blockchain**

This was the first type of blockchain to existing, and it refers to blockchains that are publicly accessible from the Internet. An example of this type of blockchain is Bitcoin, Ethereum, Dash, Monero, or Zcash. This type of blockchain keeps its data, software, and development open to the public so that anyone can review, audit, develop or improve them. Public blockchains have security measures to ensure that no malicious actor can easily tamper with the operation of the blockchain. This is where Byzantine fault tolerance in programming, robust consensus protocols, DDoS protections, or against 51% or double-spend attacks come into action. In short, any measure that helps improve network security is implemented on the network. The purpose of all this is to keep the network running and preserve its decentralization.

- **Characteristics of public blockchains**

Among the characteristics of this type of network, we can mention:

Public blockchains allow anyone to be part of it. Whether as a user, miner, or administrator of a node, people can access the network and be part of it without any restrictions. E operation of the network is completely transparent and open. Since its inception, blockchain data has been available to everyone without restrictions. Anyone can review or audit the operation of the network, and its software here is no centralized entity. Public networks are entirely decentralized, and no central authority regulates their function. The economic maintenance of the blockchain depends on the system integrated with it. Generally, this financial system depends on mining and collecting commissions for each transaction carried out within the network.

2. **Private or permissioned blockchain**

Later, with the evolution of blockchain technology and its expansion, many companies became interested in it. This led to the development of private or permissioned blockchain solutions. This type of blockchain generally has the same elements as a public blockchain, but unlike public blockchains, permissioned blockchains depend on a central unit that controls all actions within it. This main unit is what allows access to users, in addition to managing their functions and permissions within the blockchain. They are generally proprietary software development options, although there are also free software developments. One of the most critical private blockchain developments in the crypto world is Hyperledger. This project initiated by the Linux Foundation and several companies in the technology sector is the best example of private blockchain. We can also mention the case of Corda from R3 or Quorum from JPMorgan.

- **Characteristics of private blockchains**

Among the characteristics of this type of network, we can mention:

Access to the network is restricted to elements that the central control unit can only authorize

Access to the transaction book or any other means of information generated by the blockchain is private

The economic maintenance of the blockchain generally depends on the company that supports the project. Private blockchains often do not hold cryptocurrencies or mining

3. Hybrid or federated blockchain

This type of blockchain is a fusion between public and private blockchains. It is an attempt to take advantage of the best of both worlds. In these blockchains, participation in the network is private. One or more entities control access to network resources. However, the ledger is publicly accessible. This means that anyone can explore block by block everything in the blockchain.

For example, these types of blockchain networks benefit governments or business organizations that want to store or share data securely. A perfect use case happens in the health sector, where blockchain accumulates data from its drug production lines. The competent authority can review the stored data to control quality, both at the company and government levels. The goal of applying this blockchain model is to maintain a high level of transparency and trust.

- **Characteristics of hybrid or federated blockchains**

Among the attributes of this type of network, we can mention:

Access to the network is restricted to elements that the rest of the control units can only authorize

Access to the transaction book or any other means of information generated by the blockchain is public

There is no mining or cryptocurrencies. The consensus of the network is given by other means that ensure that the data is correct

It is partially decentralized, which leads to a better level of security and transparency

4. Semi-private blockchain

Last on our list of blockchain types is semi-private, which follows the consortium's idea of easing permissions. But, unlike the first, here, there is a single organization, or company, that manages the entry of members. And, unlike the private blockchain, the set of criteria is pre-established and, if followed, allows any new members to join. Therefore, we can say that it is more decentralized than the private one, but not to the point of becoming public.

Oh! This is one of the most used blockchain types by governments and business-to-business transactions.

How is a blockchain built?

Now, the blockchain's construction and operation are dependent on several factors, which we'll go through below:

> **Blocks**

A block is a collection of confirmed transactions and associated data stored in the blockchain. Each block in the chain (excluding the generating block, which starts the chain) is made up of the following components:

An alphanumeric code that refers to the block before it. It contains a package of transactions (the number determined by different factors) that will use a new alphanumeric code to link to the next block.

The currently active block attempts to calculate the third point we have mentioned. A legitimate code fulfills specific rules and can only be achieved repeatedly. But how do these blocks come to be? This is the job of the next element to investigate.

> **Miners**

Miners are specialized computers or devices that contribute computing power to the bitcoin network (also known as "mine"). This ability is used to confirm the transactions that occur. Each time someone completes a block, they are rewarded with bitcoins and a fee for each transaction processed.

> **Nodes**

A node is a computer or chip connected to the bitcoin network and runs software that keeps and distributes an up-to-date copy of the blockchain in real-time. When a block is confirmed and added to the chain, it is sent to all nodes and added to the document that each of them keeps. One of the most intriguing aspects of the bitcoin protocol is that each unit is not a file in the traditional sense; instead, each unit is sent as if it were a movie or song, in the manner of a P2P network like BitTorrent. In reality, what is produced is a record of the change of ownership of a certain number of bitcoins in the blockchain. The most common node software on the Bitcoin network is Bitcoin Core. Of course, all cryptocurrencies follow this three-part structure, each with its peculiarities. But this simple way of operating guarantees the maximum security the blockchain provides.

Advantages Of Blockchain

✦ **Reinforced security**.

Your data is sensitive and vital, and blockchain has the potential to alter how people see it drastically. By creating an immutable and end-to-end encrypted record, blockchain helps prevent fraud and unauthorized activity. Privacy issues can also be addressed on the blockchain by anonymizing personal data and user permissions to control access. The data is saved over a network of computers rather than on a single server, making it difficult for hackers to gain access.

✦ **More transparency**

Without the blockchain, each company must maintain a separate database. Because the blockchain uses a distributed ledger, transactions and data are recorded identically in multiple places. All network participants with access permission see the same information simultaneously, which sets up complete transparency. All transactions are recorded in an unmodifiable manner and are timestamped. This allows members to view the entire history of a transaction and virtually eliminates the possibility of fraud.

✦ **Instant traceability**

The blockchain creates an audit trail that documents the provenance of an asset at every stage of its journey. This blockchain audit trail serves as evidence in sectors in which consumers care about environmental issues or human rights manufacturing a product or in industries plagued by counterfeiting and fraud. With blockchain, provenance data can be shared directly with customers. Traceability data can also expose weak points in any supply chain, such as when goods are waiting at a loading dock during transit.

⚓ Increased efficiency and speed

Traditional paper-based processes are inefficient, prone to human error, and frequently necessitate a third-party mediator. Transactions may be completed faster and more efficiently using blockchain to streamline these processes. Documentation and transaction details can be recorded on the blockchain, obviating the need to exchange conventional documents. Since there is no need to synchronize multiple ledgers, posting and processing can be faster.

⚓ Automating

Transactions can even be automated using 'smart contracts, resulting in more efficient and faster processing. Once the previously specified conditions are met, the next stage of the transaction or process is triggered automatically. Smart contracts reduce human intervention and avoid relying on third parties to verify that the terms of the agreement have been met. In insurance, for example, when a customer has provided all the necessary documentation to file a claim, the action can be automatically processed and paid.

Disadvantages of Blockchain

❖ Technological heaviness

The transmission of information by the chain of blocks requires fairly significant technological support. Many computers compete to solve a series of calculations that allow encrypted information transfer: mining. The computer that solves the problem receives digital currency as a credit. But this process can be slow. A Bitcoin transaction can take up to several hours, whereas simple traditional marketing can be instantaneous (provided you pay extra to the bank). The more demand for blockchain-based devices will exploit the more computers. This will further slowdown the system. Although new, faster technological approaches like the Blockchain are beginning to be developed; such as the Tangle, this process is still prolonged.

❖ Pollution from mining farms

Mining farms were born out of this need: the more computers an individual harnesses to solve these calculations, the more likely he will be paid. But these machines must run at full speed without interruption: it consumes a lot of energy, and you have to have powerful fans. This is why mining farms have been set up in Iceland (see photo above): it is colder there, cheaper electricity, and the machines' ventilation is less expensive. The more interest in blockchain increases, the more it will be necessary to build mining farms to facilitate the growing number of operations that will need to be resolved by the minute. More farms mean more energy consumed; therefore, more pollution linked to this production.

❖ Intellectual inaccessibility

If, in theory, the usefulness and operation of the blockchain still seem accessible to the general public, in practice, it is another story. The addresses of the blocks are hashes, i.e., sequences of characters including numbers and letters, which, for the majority of individuals, do not represent much. Before using this complex technology, you have to sacrifice a lot of your time to understand its actual usefulness. Those who understand how to handle them will have an advantage over others. They can – and do – create simplified applications to manage the blockchain. Applications that they will charge for those who wish to use them.

❖ Endorsement By an Authority

Not all administrative processes can be replaced by blockchain technology. Some still require the approval of a competent authority. Certain operations that would be carried out via the blockchain – without any intermediary, therefore – would thus have no value. The Swiss newspaper Le Temps gives the example of property transfers. "The transferred contract must take the authentic form (notary) and be verified by the keeper of the land register. The newspaper writes that a real estate transaction that only goes through the blockchain has no value," writes the newspaper.

❖ Unemployment increase

Due to its simplicity and automation, the blockchain could replace many fund, accounting, and administrative services and eliminate many professions. Blockchain technology could send many employees out of work: bankers, accountants, insurers, notaries, and civil servants. There are, therefore, as many advantages as disadvantages to using the blockchain. Some think it will revolutionize the industrial and economic world. Others think it's a waste of time. The future will decide.

❖ Inefficient

Blockchains, particularly those that use Proof of Work, are inefficient. Because mining is very competitive, with only one winner every ten minutes, all other miners' efforts are wasted. Because miners are constantly trying to improve their computational power to increase their chances of finding a valid block hash, the Bitcoin network's resources have grown significantly in recent years. It now consumes more energy than many countries.

How will blockchain change the way we do business?

To understand the potential of blockchain, it is necessary to know the concept of "smart contracts." These contracts establish how code-driven agreements work and perform data exchanges. The good old vending machine is the forerunner of the smart contract, a pioneer in blockchain, in a paper written for the Chamber of Digital Commerce. These machines are security mechanisms. The value stored in the safe must be less than the cost to break into it. In addition, the device reflects the nature of the transaction, computing and releasing the change and removing the requested product by the client.

He says that smart contracts can reduce the costs of calculating complex results, making contracts that were not possible before. For example, in companies that maintain many records of business transactions, smart contracts can digitize the Uniform Business Code filing and automate renewal and release processes.

For companies that transfer goods between countries, blockchain can speed up the creation of the letter of credit and the beginning of the payment process and provide more liquidity to financial assets.

For financial organizations, smart contracts make it possible to create accurate and transparent records of financial data across organizations, which improves the ability to generate financial reports and lowers audit and insurance costs. In addition, smart contracts can provide visibility into all stages of the supply chain. Through the IoT, devices can change intelligent contracts as a product moves from the factory to the store, providing real-time visibility into a company's supply chain.

Blockchain Technology Key Use Cases

Many sectors can benefit from the use cases exposed above. This section will see specific examples of Blockchain use cases in different sectors (including advertising, insurance, real estate, energy, and activities such as record management) that highlight the effectiveness of this disruptive technology.

How to Invest in Blockchain Technology

Combining blockchain technology with equities can be a lucrative investment, and there are various ways to begin your first blockchain investment. Bitcoin is frequently the first thing that comes to mind when investing in blockchain technology, and it should not be overlooked. Apart from Bitcoin, cryptocurrency penny stocks like Altcoin and Litecoin can also be purchased. A few applications and administrations are in the beginning phases of advancement and are raising support utilizing blockchain innovation. Investing in blockchain-based firms is another way to get involved with the technology. Finally, investing in blockchain technology in its purest form is always an option.

- ✓ **A blockchain wallet:** It is a digital wallet that holds and manages cryptocurrencies such as Bitcoin, Ether, and others. The wallet service supplied by Blockchain, a software business founded by Peter Smith and Nicolas Cary, is also known as Blockchain Wallet.

- ✓ **Understanding Blockchain Wallet**

  Individuals can use e-wallets to hold bitcoins and other digital assets. Users of Blockchain Wallet may manage their cryptocurrency balances, including widely-known Bitcoin and Ether and stellar, Tether, and Paxos Standard. The procedure of creating an e-wallet with a Blockchain Wallet is entirely free, and the account creation is completed entirely online. People should supply an email address and secret word that will be utilized to deal with the record, and the framework will send a mechanized email mentioning that the document is confirmed. When the wallet is made, the client is given a Wallet ID, a unique identifier like a ledger number.2 Wallet holders can get to their e-wallet by signing into the Blockchain site or downloading and contacting a versatile application.

✓ **Advertising**

Transparency from the buyer's point of view: Blockchain for audits. From the seller's point of view of Verification of reproductions (PoV – Proof-of-View) to fight against fraud. The mechanisms for calculating PoV reproductions only consider the viewings of authenticated users since the unique identifier of each user is part of the information necessary to believe that a replica is valid. Given that most people can only consume audiovisual content one at a time, PoV mechanisms discount the views of those users who play (via streaming) several videos simultaneously. PoV technology confirms playing a video by capturing randomly chosen frames for playback duration. Intelligent contracts can document the number of reproductions and processes and determine the corresponding payments.

✓ **Insurance**

Probably the best Blockchain application in the insurance field is smart contracts. According to Deloitte, the use of contracts supported by distributed registry technologies would allow claims to be managed in a truly transparent and secure way, both for clients and insurers. Warrants and shares would be registered on the Blockchain platform and validated by the network, eliminating any claims that were not valid. For example, the blockchain would reject multiple lawsuits related to the same accident. BBVA-Open Mind-Banafa-REal State-Key Blockchain Use Cases-avi-Waxman-Blockchain would offer transparency throughout the entire selling and purchasing process blockchain would offer complete transparency in the whole buying and selling process.

✓ **Real estate**

On average, an owner or owner changes houses every five or seven years, while, on average, a person will move houses about twelve times during his life. Blockchain technology can become a handy tool for the real estate market, given the volume of transactions. It would speed up sales by offering a quick way to check the parties' financial situation. It would reduce fraud cases thanks to its encryption features and guarantee the transparency of the entire buying and selling process.

✓ **Energy sector**

Can use blockchain technology to execute electricity supply transactions, but it could also offer the starting point to develop meter reading applications and billing and compensation management. Could also use it to develop applications for documentation of ownership, asset management, guarantees of origin, and renewable energy and emission quotas. BBVA-Open Mind-Key Blockchain Use Cases-Record Management nana-Smirnova-Blockchain technology can simplify this record keeping. Blockchain technology can help simplify record keeping.

✓ **Records Management**

The regional, regional, and state governments are responsible for maintaining the records of individuals, including dates of birth and death, marital status, or property transfers. Managing all this information is not an easy task. In addition, today, some of these records only exist in physical format. This implies making any change in person, which entails inconvenience, time spent, and inefficiencies. Blockchain technology can help simplify the maintenance of these types of records.

How Blockchain Wallet Works

Clients can send a solicitation to one more party for a particular measure of bitcoin or other crypto-resources. The system delivers an extraordinary area that can be sent off an outcast or changed over into a Quick feedback code or QR code for short code. A QR code is like a scanner tag, which stores financial data and can be perused by a computerized gadget.

Each time a user makes a request, a unique address is produced. Users can send crypto assets when they are given an individual lesson. The send-and-receive process is identical to sending or receiving funds via PayPal, except that bitcoin is used instead of PayPal. PayPal is a form of online payment system that acts as a go-between for consumers and their banks and credit cards, enabling online transfers. Users can swap

Bitcoin for other crypto-assets and vice versa using swapping. This method is a straightforward way to trade crypto without jeopardizing the security of your Blockchain Wallet. Users are given a rate of how much money they will receive based on the current exchange rate, which changes depending on how long it takes them to complete the transaction. While the transactions are added to each currency's blockchain, swaps should take a couple of hours. Users should contact customer service if it takes more than six hours. Blockchain Wallet supports only six crypto-assets: Bitcoin, Ethereum, Bitcoin Cash, Stellar Lumens, Tether, USD Digital, and Wrapped-DGLD. To make a buy, a client can either move assets from a bank, utilize a credit or charge card, or use the accessible money balance.10 There is an everyday cutoff of $25,000 and a week-by-week breaking point of $100,000 as well as a base purchase request of $5 and the most significant purchase request of $25,000.11

✓ **Blockchain Wallet Fees**

However, it's worth noting that the Blockchain Wallet employs a mechanism known as dynamic pricing, which means that the cost charged per transaction might vary depending on various factors. The charge is influenced by the transaction size and the network parameters at the transaction time. Miners are powerful computers that can only handle a fixed number of transactions every block. Miners usually execute the trades with the highest fees first since they are more profitable. Blockchain Wallet offers a need expense, which might get the exchange handled soon. Additionally, there's a standard charge, which is less expensive, yet the sale would almost certainly take over 60 minutes. The client can likewise alter expenses. Notwithstanding, on the off chance that the client sets the payment too low, the exchange or exchange could be deferred or rejected.

✓ Blockchain Wallet Security

Clients should be worried about wallet security because a compromised record could bring about them failing to keep a grip on their resources. Blockchain Wallet includes various insurance degrees to get client cash from any likely aggressor, including the actual organization.

✓ Passwords

Like other advanced administrations, Blockchain Wallet accounts require passwords for the clients' insurance. Notwithstanding, the Blockchain organization doesn't store client passwords and can't reset the secret word whenever lost. This action keeps organization insiders from having the option to take digital currencies. Assuming that a client neglects or fails their secret phrase, the record must be recuperated with a mental helper seed.

✓ Mnemonic Seeds

A memory aide seed is an arbitrary line of English words that fills in as a secret phrase substitute. The seed can be utilized to reestablish the wallet, including any bitcoins, assuming a client loses admittance to their telephone or gadget. The Blockchain firm does not put away clients' mental helper seeds, similar to passwords. The wallets can be recuperated regardless of whether the organization leaves the business because these seeds adhere to an industry guideline.

✓ Future of Blockchain

Without question, the benefits of Blockchain technology will entice businesses and organizations all over the world to invest more in it. Although it's still in early stages, this, one of the most recent technologies, will take some time to gain traction and will necessitate patience. However, the benefits of Blockchain are difficult to overlook, and the technology will undoubtedly benefit a variety of businesses since the Verification of every piece of data that enters and exits these Blockchain systems will mitigate many risks.

✓ **Future of Blockchain in the Finance Industry**

When it comes to tracking financial assets, Blockchain technology has delivered on its promises and demonstrated consistency. After seeing the potential and benefits of this technology, several financial institutions decided to invest in it. Blockchain can combat the flow and deals of black money because of its transparent ledger structure. Governments are exploring it as a way to improve the efficiency of their economies' rules.

✓ **Future of Blockchain in Cybersecurity**

Blockchain technology's future potential is mostly in the sphere of cybersecurity, for obvious reasons. The data is protected and verifiable, despite the fact that the Blockchain ledger is open and dispersed. To eliminate risks such as illegal data manipulation, the encryption is done using cryptography.

✓ **Blockchain in Cloud Storage**

Data hacking, loss, and human mistake are all risks associated with centralized systems. Cloud storage may be made more secure and resistant to hacking by implementing Blockchain technology, just as it can be in cybersecurity.

✓ **Blockchain in IoT and Networking**

Blockchain technology is being used by companies like IBM and Samsung to create a distributed network of IoT devices. The concept is known as ADEPT, and it intends to eliminate the need for a centralized site to coordinate communication between devices for tasks such as software upgrades, error handling, energy conservation, and so on.

✓ **Use of Blockchain in Digital Advertising**

Due to the difficulties that digital advertising faces, such as bot traffic, lack of transparency, domain fraud, inefficient payment processes, and so on, promoters and publishers are having a difficult time due to unethical actors. Blockchain has been discovered to overcome such supply chain difficulties due to its transparency and trustworthiness. Using this technology, advertising-related transactions can be handled more efficiently.

NFT: THE NEW WAY OF CREATING AND SELLING ART

Introduction

We live in a strange world, a place where the virtual becomes more and more tangible, not precisely because we bring them to reality. On the contrary, we are drawn into his plane. Thanks to this transformation, today, we make possible things like NFTs and the multi-million-dollar sale of digital art.

It could not be in another, but in our weird world, where a person pays thousands of dollars and only receives "code" in return. Not a sculpture, not a file, not even a copy of the piece you bought. Just a code. A succession of numbers and letters that designate you as the owner of something that everyone can see for free.

NFTs are perhaps much easier to understand for those who have dealt with cryptocurrencies before. Using similar logic, they make it possible to designate provable ownership of an asset on the Internet. A work of art, for example.

The technical explanation of NFTs

The Non-Fungible Tokens are part of the Blockchain world where taking cryptocurrencies such as Bitcoin as an example, NFTs are Tokens that cannot be copied, that is, there will only be one piece or limited pieces in the world, in the case that it is a collection like in Pokemon cards where there can be 100 copies, there will only be 100 copies and no more. In addition to the fact that the Blockchain is practically impossible to hack or modify due to the whole issue of security and decentralized data.

WHAT ARE NFTS?

NFT is nothing more than the acronym used in English to refer to the Non-Fungible Token, which is digital files that cannot be altered or duplicated. In other words: they are unique, original, and of an exceptional rarity.

Files designated as NFTs typically have a history or added value behind them, either because of their origin or their characteristics. It can be practically anything on the web, but currently, its boom is due to its use in the art world.

Let us imagine the following example, to which we are already accustomed. A billionaire buys a work of art for his personal collection. He can put it on display, share it on Instagram, or even take a selfie with it, but it's still his.

Although everyone can see it, he remains the undisputed owner. Depending on its market value, you can sell it, exchange it, or use it as a form of payment to acquire a greater good.

Using blockchain technology, NFTs make it possible for anyone on the Internet to legally and provably buy or sell ownership of a work. This property may increase or decrease in value, just as investment assets do in the real world.

One of the most famous anecdotes on the subject is that of Nyan Cat, the viral animation created by Chris Torres in 2011. Being an essential part of the history of the Internet, it was sold for $600,000.

Why do NFTs have value?

Scarcity and unique pieces

Everything in society has a value given by the society itself; we return to the example of Bitcoin where society and early adopters have given it that value from zero to what it is worth today ($55,000) for 1 bitcoin. The

Millennials and Generation Z market are full of technology, so thinking about this market and the ease that the digital world gives you, artists, musicians, writers, designers, producers, and influencers are seeing a business opportunity fascinating and growing.

Certificate of authenticity and digital seal (signature)

All NFTs are protected by the Blockchain and its decentralized data system, in addition to each work bearing the stamp (signature) of the original author who owns the work (NFT).

You don't just collect; you can invest and sell.

When an NFT is launched, it is launched at an initial price or with an auction that closes at a final price but does not end there; the buyer can decide whether to keep that NFT (work) in their collection or put it up for sale for a highest price and the original owner who sold it for the first price will continually earn a royalty on each transaction.

PERSONALITIES SELLING NFTs

Beeple sold an NFT for $69 million

Digital artist Mike Winkelmann (@beeple) sold his first 5,000 pieces of art collaged into a gigantic JPG for just $69 Million. You can see the work and give it a super zoom from here.

Willyrex prepares its first NFTs

Willyrex Youtuber Gamer is preparing his exit to the NFTs to start selling from €1 euro. He hopes his collection will become so famous that when his works are resold for millions of dollars, he will take 5% of each transaction, no matter how many.

Platzi has NFTs for sale

Platzi, the Hispanic Online Education Startup, put up for sale a mural designed by its internal team, where anyone can buy a part of that mural and even the entire mural.

How to create, buy and sell NFTs

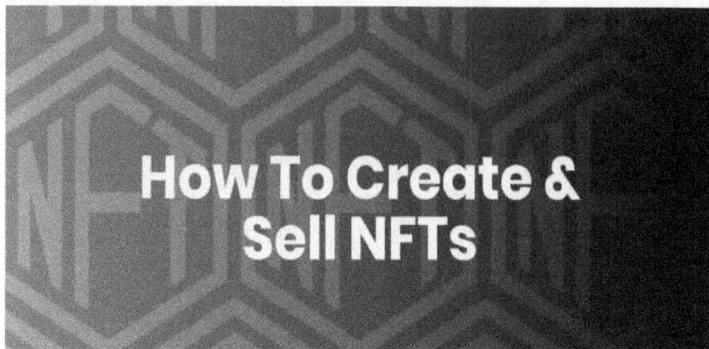

How To Create & Sell NFTs

With total sales increasing by 55% from $250 million to $389 million in 2021, NFTs have become one of the most popular cryptocurrency trends. These popular digital assets can be created, bought, and sold in the following ways.

Non-fungible tokens (NFT), which are characterized as one-of-a-kind collectible crypto assets, have been around since 2012, when the concept of bitcoin-colored coins (BTC, -0.56%), also known as colored coins in English, first emerged. These coins were simply satoshis—small fractions of a bitcoin—with unique information that could be linked to real-world assets. "This satoshi is $500 from the John Doe office building in New York," I used to be able to say. The vast majority of colored coins, on the other hand, were used to create and trade works of art on Counterparty, a peer-to-peer trading platform based on the Blockchain, such as "Rare Pepe" digital cards.

These frog cartoons were among the first examples of original digital artwork linked to cryptocurrency tokens based on a popular internet meme. This laid down the way to create new non-fungible token standards, which are a set of blockchain building blocks that enable developers to develop non-fungible tokens of their design.

NFTs can be used to illustrate any tangible or intangible object, such as:

- Artworks
- Video games Items like Skins, Weapons, Virtual currency, and Avatars
- Music
- Collectible items (digital cards, for example)
- Real-World Assets Tokenized: From Real Estate and Automobiles to Racehorses and Designer Sneakers
- Virtual Terrain

- Videos of thrilling sporting events

How to create NFTs

Creating your own NFT, whether it's a GIF or an image, is a relatively simple process that doesn't necessitate extensive cryptocurrency knowledge. NFT works can also be turned into collectibles like digital card sets.

First, it would be best to decide which Blockchain you want to use to create your NFTs. For the time being, Ethereum is the most popular blockchain platform for issuing NFTs. Nonetheless, there is a range of other blockchains that are becoming increasingly popular:

- Binance Smart Chain
- Flow by Dapper Labs
- Tron

- eos (EOS, -1.50%)
- Polkadot
- Tezos
- Cosmos
- WAX

The NFT token standard supported wallet services and marketplaces are unique to each Blockchain. If you make NFTs on Binance Smart Chain, you can only sell them on platforms that accept Binance Smart Chain assets, and this means you won't be able to trade them on VIV3, a Flow blockchain-based exchange, or OpenSea, an Ethereum-based NFT exchange.

Since Ethereum has the largest ecosystem of NFTs, here's what you'll need to mint your artwork, music, or video on it:

An Ethereum wallet that supports ERC-721 —the Ethereum-based NFT token standard—includes MetaMask, Trust Wallet, or Coinbase Wallet.

Between $50 and $100 in ethereum (ETH, -1.15%) (ETH). If you use the Coinbase wallet, you can buy ether from the platform with US dollars, British pounds, and other fiat currencies. If not, you will have to buy ether on a cryptocurrency exchange. You can find here a guide to buy cryptocurrencies using the most popular exchanges.

Once you have all of this, you can connect your wallet to several NFT-focused platforms and upload the image or file you want to convert into a non-fungible token.

The main Ethereum NFT markets are:

- OpenSea
- Rarible
- Mintable

Makersplace also allows you to create your own NFTs, but you have to pre-register to be a listed artist on the platform.

OpenSea, Rarible, and Mintable have a "Create" button in the top right corner. The process works at OpenSea, currently the largest Ethereum-based NFT marketplace.

When you click the "Create" button, a screen will appear asking you to connect your Ethereum wallet. It will connect to the marketplace once you have entered your wallet password. To prove that you own the address on your Ethereum wallet, you may need to sign a message digitally, but it only takes one click to do so.

It costs nothing to sign a message digitally; it simply proves that you are the wallet owner.

The next step in OpenSea is to select "My Collections" from the top right corner. Click the blue "Create" button.

You'll be directed to a window where you can upload your artwork, name it, and give it a description.

This section focuses on creating a folder for your newly formed NFTs. When you've assigned an image to a collection, it'll appear in the example below (blue). After that, click the pencil icon in the top right corner to add a header image to the page (red).

In OpenSea, add a banner image to the NFT collection.

Your page should resemble the illustration below. If that's the case, you're ready to make your first NFT. Sign another message with your wallet by clicking the "Add New Item" button (blue).

You will come to a new window where you can upload your NFT image, audio, GIF, or 3D model.

You can also include unique traits and attributes to increase the scarcity and uniqueness of your NFT on OpenSea and many other marketplaces. Even better, creators can create unlockable content that only the buyer can see. It could be anything, from passwords to specific services to promotional codes and contact information.

Characteristics of an NFT on the OpenSea platform.

When you're finished, click "Create" at the bottom and confirm the NFT's creation by signing another message in your wallet. After that, the work should appear in your collection.

How to create and put up for sale an NFT in 7 easy steps?

You can do it without difficulty if you are an artist or simply want to experiment with this new technology. Look over the steps outlined below.

1. Define the utility of the NFTs you want to create

The first thing you should do is define the utility of the NFTs you wish to create. Because yes, NFTs must have some associated utility. Or be excellent art, of course.

Some NFTs have an artistic value by themselves, either because of their quality or because they are the first or have meant some milestone. But, if you're not going to create outstanding art or anything milestone, you need to offer some utility.

What kind of utility?

There are many types. For example, you can create a community with certain benefits for being part of it. You can also commit to developing the intellectual property of those NFTs. Or you can raise future projects in which the holders of those NFTs you take out first may prioritize participating.

2. Determine the art (and create it)

The next step is to determine the type of art you will create. Maybe you are an exceptional artist, and you already have different pieces that you want to turn into NFTs. Or perhaps you're not, and you want to start a collection to make money from this NFT boom.

Both options are acceptable. But, if you are in the second group, you must determine the art and create it.

You are probably wondering how it is possible that there are people who create 4000 pieces of art and put them up for sale. These art pieces are not made one by one, but rather a system is known as a procedural generation.

Basically, some elements are taken, and, based on them, the different NFTs are systematically created, permuting the various factors that can make up the work.

Whether you want a collection of unique pieces or if you want to create an enormous collection with a procedural system, you must have a good artist (if it is you, great, but if not, you will have to find one and pay for their Job). The point is that you have to determine the art and create it before you create the NFT itself.

3. Create an Ethereum wallet

The next step is to create an Ethereum wallet for yourself. In order to be able to mint an NFT (minting is the verb for "adding an NFT to the blockchain"), you need to have one of these wallets, even if you don't have Ethereum in it (although the latter will depend on the marketplace you use – in the case that let's put us, the one from OpenSea, you don't need to have Ethereum in the wallet).

We recommend MetaMask. It's free and easy to get and use.

4. Connect to OpenSea

When you have your wallet, you will have to connect to OpenSea. OpenSea is the central Marketplace for NFTs and allows you to create them right there.

It will catch your attention that it is no longer necessary to create an account and log in to this type of website. No way! That has already been replaced by a connection to your wallet (to your MetaMask, in this case). Much faster and more efficient.

Future websites will work this way, so get used to it.

5. Complete the form

Once you are connected, you can click on "Create" and start the process of creating your NFT. There is no loss: all you have to do is fill in the different sections that it asks you.

The vast majority of these fields have to do with the characteristics of your NFT, but there is one that is especially important. It is about "Blockchain." Through this section, you choose the Blockchain where you want to mint your NFT. Choose wisely!

6. Create it

With the above, you will have all the sections of your NFT ready. All you have to do is create it, determine its sale price (or starting price, if you choose the auction option), and you're done. You already have your first NFT.

And it didn't cost you a single euro! Of course, when you sell it, OpenSea will take a commission. In fact, the reality is that until someone buys your NFT, you don't have an NFT as such. Only at the time of purchase is it lied.

7. **Promote it**

To finish, you have the most crucial thing left... Sell your NFT! If you expected that, buyers would come and take it from your hands just by creating it. I am sorry to tell you that it is more likely that you will win the lottery.

So, you are going to have to do marketing, promote it and get people interested in what you have created. Only then will you sell your NFT.

As you can see, creating your own NFT and putting it up for sale is really easy. If you follow the steps we have mentioned, you can have your NFT up and running in just a few minutes.

Of course, whether or not you sell will depend on a thousand factors, such as the quality of your artwork and what you offer along with the NFT. And, of course, the publicity you make of it.

How much does it cost to make NFT?

Although creating NFTs on OpenSea is free, some platforms charge a fee. This fee is referred to as "gas" in Ethereum-based systems, and it simply refers to the amount of ether needed to perform a specific function on the Blockchain, such as adding a new NFT to the marketplace. Gas prices vary according to network congestion. The higher the price of gas, the more people on the network transacting value transactions at any given time. And the other way around.

Tip: During the weekend, when fewer people transact on the network, Ethereum gas fees are significantly lower than average. If you're selling multiple NFTs, this can help you save money.

How to sell NFTs?

To sell your NFTs on a marketplace, go to your collection, click on them, and then click the "Sell" button. By clicking on it, you'll be taken to a pricing page where you can specify the transaction's terms, including whether you want an auction or a fixed-price sale.

Ether and other ERC-20 tokens are the most common cryptocurrencies for which you can sell your NFTs. On the other hand, some platforms only support the native token of the Blockchain on which they were built. VIV3, for example, is a marketplace that only accepts FLOW tokens and is built on the FLOW blockchain.

By selecting the "Edit" button next to the collection image on OpenSea, approving the message with your wallet, and scrolling down, you can schedule royalties and select which ERC-20 token you want to receive for the collection's sale. NFT Royalties enable NFT creators to earn a commission each time the asset is sold to a new buyer. This can potentially create lifetime passive income streams for artists and other content creators automatically, thanks to smart contracts.

Posting NFTs on the market sometimes requires a fee to complete the process. Although this is not the case for all platforms, it is something to consider when creating NFTs.

How to buy NFTs

Before rushing to buy NFTs, there are four things to consider:

- In which marketplace do you intend to buy the NFTs
- Which wallet do you need to download to connect to the platform and buy NFTs?
- What cryptocurrency do you need to fund your wallet with to complete the sale?

- Whether the NFTs you want to buy are sold at a particular time or through an auction.

As you might expect, some NFTs are only available on specific platforms. You'll need to open an NBA Top Shot account, create a Dapper wallet, and fund it with the USDC stablecoin or one of the supported fiat currencies to buy NBA Top Shot packs. You'll also have to wait for one of the card pack deliveries to be announced, and I hope that you'll be able to get one before they run out.

"Pack drops" and "art drops" are becoming more popular ways of selling rare NFTs to a large audience of eager buyers. Users are usually required to sign up and fund their accounts ahead of time to not miss out on purchasing NFTs when they run out. The "pack drops" and "art drops" can end in seconds, so you have to have everything prepared beforehand.

Where to buy NFTs

Here is a list of the most popular marketplaces in 2021 for crypto traders who are primarily interested in buying NFTs:

- OpenSea
- Rarible
- SuperRare
- Nifty Gateway
- Foundation
- Axie Marketplace
- BakerySwap
- NFT ShowRoom
- VIV3

Is now a good time to buy NFTs?

The NFT craze is far from over. The UFC and Shawn Mendez, for example, have signed deals to launch their own non-expendable assets soon. Grimes, Elon Musk's girlfriend, has joined the movement, selling nearly $6 million in digital artwork in just minutes.

As more artists, brands, and icons flock to the space to create their own unique tokens, Messari analyst Mason

Nystrom expects the NFT market to exceed $1.3 billion by the end of 2021. This is an excellent time to get involved in the space, with more blockchains competing to produce better NFT services and a growing number of platforms to choose from.

DEFI IS THE NEW BANKING

What is decentralized finance (Defi)?

Decentralized finance (Defi) is an umbrella term for various public blockchain applications and projects to disrupt the traditional finance world. Defi is defined as financial applications built on blockchain technologies, typically using smart contracts, and is inspired by blockchain technology. Smart contracts are automated enforceable agreements that can be accessed by anyone with an internet connection and do not require intermediaries to execute.

Defi refers to applications and peer-to-peer protocols built on decentralized blockchain networks that do not require access rights for simple lending, borrowing, or trading of financial tools. The Ethereum network makes most Defi applications today, but many alternative public networks are emerging that provide superior speed, scalability, security, and lower costs.

How did Defi get its start?

Initially, humans bartered for goods and services. However, as humans evolved, so did economies: we invented currency to facilitate the exchange of goods and services. As a result, coins aided in introducing innovations and developing higher economic levels. Progress, however, comes at a cost.

Historically, central governments have issued currencies that underpin our economies, giving them more power as more people came to trust them. However, trust has been broken occasionally, leading people to question the centralized authorities' ability to manage the money. Defi was founded to develop a financial system that is open to all and reduces the need to trust and rely on a central authority.

Defi, according to some, began in 2009 with the introduction of Bitcoin, the first peer-to-peer digital currency built on top of the blockchain network. Because of Bitcoin, the concept of ushering transformation into the traditional financial world via blockchains has become an essential next step in decentralizing legacy economic systems. All of this is thanks to the 2015 launch of Ethereum and, more specifically, smart contracts. The Ethereum network is a second-generation blockchain that fully realizes the financial industry's potential with this technology. In addition, it encouraged businesses and enterprises to create and deploy Defi-related projects, forming the Defi ecosystem.

Defi provided a wealth of chances to create a transparent and robust financial system that a single company does not control. However, the turning point for financial applications began in 2017, with initiatives enabling more functionalities than only money transmission.

How Defi works

Devi, also known as "open finance," eliminates the need for an intermediary in financial transactions. So, instead of having your bank or credit card company function as a middleman between you and a retailer when you make a transaction, you utilize digital currency and own it directly. Defi is founded mainly on

Ethereum, the second most popular cryptocurrency after Bitcoin.

The following are the central Defi tenets:

- Because there are no intermediaries, your funds are not in the hands of banks or institutions.
- There is some transparency because the code is available for anyone to review.
- There are open networks that span geographical boundaries.
- Numerous applications are available for users, primarily based on Ethereum.

Though Defi is frequently mentioned in cryptocurrency, it goes beyond creating a new digital currency or value. Instead, Devi's intelligent contracts aim to replace the role of traditional financial systems.

"It's all about code in Defi. Your money is programmed to perform various [functions] with the help of smart contracts. It provides a one-of-a-kind opportunity for anyone with a computer and an internet connection to participate in the global economy, "Mozgovoy adds.

One of the most appealing aspects of Defi is that it eliminates the entry barrier for many of these financial transactions. You don't have a government or corporation managing your money, and you don't have to meet specific financial requirements.

You apply for a loan using traditional financial systems and may be rejected based on your credit. For example, you have a bank account or an investment brokerage account with a company that manages your funds.

After certain conditions are met, specific financial transactions are carried out using DeFi's smart contracts. For example, smart contracts make borrowing, lending, and other transactions possible, and the transaction terms are written in the code. Unfortunately, while this makes these transactions more convenient and efficient, they can also be more vulnerable.

Because of these smart contracts and the ability for Ethereum to create applications, Defi can be used:

As a peer-to-peer lending network, it provides peer-to-peer borrowing and lending. Users can exchange one type of currency for another using decentralized exchange. Trading ether for US dollars, for example. For betting, users wager on the potential outcomes of specific events. As stablecoins, which link a type of cryptocurrency to a more traditional currency, such as the US dollar, reduce price volatility and increase stability.

The protocol layer defines the protocols or guidelines for intelligent contracts. The application layer is responsible for bringing the protocols to life through a consumer-facing user interface. The aggregation layer comprises aggregators who connect the various apps and protocols that serve as the foundation for borrowing, lending, and other financial services.

The benefits of decentralized finance

The Defi movement promises a slew of advantages for customers and investors, including the elimination of intermediaries and central oversight, increased access to financial markets for retail investors, and the creation of new investment opportunities. In addition, Defi developers are leveraging some fundamental properties of blockchain technology to achieve their lofty goals.

- **Permissionless**

The term "decentralized finance" already indicates what the Defi movement considers to be its defining feature. That's not surprising. The value proposition of blockchain is based on decentralization. The goal is to wean ourselves off of relying on corporations and other institutions for oversight, server space, data storage, and so on. Blockchain networks accomplish this by ensuring that all members have access to the same transaction history.

Most Defi apps are based on Ethereum, the second-largest blockchain protocol after Bitcoin. Ethereum, as a permissionless (public) blockchain, is highly decentralized and easily accessible to anyone interested in developing or deploying a Defi app. Furthermore, the blockchain's permissionless nature, as well as the interoperability it enables, opens the door to a plethora of third-party integrations.

It should be noted that these features are not unique to Ethereum. However, as the leading network for innovative contract development, Ethereum has established itself as the preferred platform for developing Defi apps and other types of decentralized apps (dApps).

- **Transparency**

Greater transparency comes with decentralization. Because the distributed ledger containing information about all the activities on a blockchain network is shared, the network's data is publicly accessible for inspection. Furthermore, the cryptographic principles that underpin blockchain ensure that information is only recorded after its authenticity has been verified.

Customers may find the transparency provided by Defi applications to be game-changing. Improving due diligence can help people identify and avoid potential financial scams and harmful business practices.

- **Immutability**

Blockchain technology achieves true immutability through the clever use of cryptography and consensus algorithms such as proof-of-work. This makes it nearly impossible to manipulate records stored on a blockchain network. When combined with the previously mentioned features, this creates a level of security that is difficult, if not impossible, to achieve through traditional means.

Defi apps bring the inherent benefits of blockchain to the financial sector while also striving to create user-friendly interfaces to ensure a positive user experience. Furthermore, smart contracts, such as dApps, protect against bad actors and fraudulent transactions.

How can DeFi help the financial services sector?

Based on what we've seen thus far, Defi has the potential to benefit traditional finance. However, as with any transformative technology, DeFi's potential extends beyond simply improving the current state of affairs. However, its true strength lies in its ability to disrupt the space by enabling new financial products and services. Even at this early stage, the technology shows promise in this regard. It is already altering how people manage their assets, borrow and lend money, and conduct online trading. Here are just a few of Devi's most notable applications:

- **Lending and borrowing**

Defi has enabled the development of peer-to-peer lending and borrowing solutions with significant end-user benefits. These services include cryptographic verification mechanisms and intelligent contract integration, eliminating the need for intermediaries like banks to verify and process lending and borrowing transactions. This makes the process much cheaper and faster while still protecting the counterparties involved in a transaction. Other advantages include speedier transaction settlement and greater accessibility.

Among the most popular Defi applications are lending and borrowing dApps. The Compound is one platform that has grown in popularity in this category. Lenders on the platform can supply crypto assets to some lending pools from which other people can borrow. Because of this, these lenders are entitled to a portion of the interest that borrowers payback to the collection. A lender's interest rate is determined by their contribution to the pool and the liquidity of the crypto assets.

- **Savings**

People can now manage their savings in new ways thanks to the growing popularity of Defi lending platforms. As previously stated, users begin earning interest on their crypto assets by locking them into lending protocols such as Compound. This has resulted in the emergence of Defi saving apps that can connect to various lending protocols to maximize their users' ability to earn interest. As a result, the term 'yield farming' has been coined to describe the increasingly popular practice of users moving their idle crypto assets around in various lending protocols to maximize returns.

Dharma, Argent, and Pool Together are three of the most popular savings apps available today.

- **Tokenization**

The recent Ethereum boom resulted in one of blockchain's most important trends – tokenization. The Protocol's powerful, innovative contract capabilities enabled the creation of crypto tokens, which are digital assets that exist on a blockchain and can have various properties and uses. These include utility tokens that are native to a specific dApp. These security tokens function similarly to digital shares, real estate tokens that allow for fractional ownership of physical properties, and others.

Tokens can also provide physical and digital assets such as oil, gold, fiat currencies, and cryptocurrencies. Tokens locked into Ethereum-based intelligent contracts serve as collateral for these so-called crypto synthetic assets. Synthetix, one of the most popular synthetic asset platforms, currently has nearly $600 million in assets under management.

- **Stablecoins**

Stablecoins, similar to synthetic crypto assets, are crypto tokens linked to stable support or a basket of assets. Stablecoins are typically pegged to fiat currencies such as the US dollar, but they can also be commodity-pegged or cryptocurrency-pegged tokens. Stablecoins aim to reduce cryptocurrency price volatility and strengthen the case for using blockchains as payment solutions.

We can categorize stablecoins into three types based on the method used to keep their value stable. Collateralized stablecoins necessitate the coin issuer holding the assets to which their coin is pegged (fiat currency, gold, silver, etc.). Other coins are linked to cryptocurrencies, preserving their value through over-collateralization and stability mechanisms.

Finally, non-collateralized tokens whose prices are algorithmically maintained at predetermined levels.

Stablecoins are what power the Defi engine in many ways. For example, they're commonly employed to facilitate remittance, lending and borrowing, and other Defi services.

- **Marketplaces**

Defi is also beginning to influence how we exchange products and services online. The recent advent of decentralized exchanges (DEXes), which enable peer-to-peer trading of digital assets, illustrates this. Again, Uniswap is a critical player in this sector.

The notion is easily extended to incorporate traditional financial instruments, physical items, and services. For example, one of Limechain's clients is developing a new way for consumers to buy smart contracts and other blockchain capabilities.

Coins associated with Defi?

Aave – AAVE

Total Supply: 16,000,000 AAVE

Aave is a leading lending protocol that secures the Protocol and participates in governance by using a native token AAVE. Aave is migrating from LEND to AAVE at a 100:1 rate, which you can monitor via the Migration Portal. Additionally, AAVE can be staked for AAVE rewards via the Safety Module.

Total Synthetix – SNX

Supply: 190,075,446

Synthetix is a leading derivatives protocol backed by the SNX native token. To create new derivatives, known as Synths, users must stake at least 750 per cent of the Synths value in SNX. Maintaining this ratio, known as a ratio, allows users to earn native inflation and a pro-rata portion of Synthetix Exchange trading fees.

YEarn – YFI

Total Supply: 30,000 YFI

yEarn is an automated liquidity aggregator that provides various yield farming opportunities. A native token governs the Protocol, YFI, released without a premise and an Initial DEX Offering. Users can stake YFI to participate in governance and receive a pro-rata share of protocol fees.

Uniswap – UNI

The total supply is 1,000,000,000 UNI.

The most prominent Defi decentralized exchange is Uniswap. Uniswap airdropped 15% of its supply to former consumers in mid-September as part of a scheme called 'Universal Basic Income.' UNI is now earned by providing liquidity to certain pools and will be utilized for governance once a more significant portion of the supply is distributed.

Swap Sushi – SUSHI

There is 250,000,000 SUSHI in total stock.

SUSHI is the governance token for the Sushiswap AMM and lending system. LPs gain it by providing liquidity to specific Sushiswap pairs, and it can be staked through the Omaske bar to earn protocol fees and issuance. SUSHI is also utilized to vote on new Onsen launch partners and projects that gain additional SUSHI awards for performing an Initial Public Offering (IPO).

Compound – COMP

Total Supply: 10,000,000 COMP

Users earn COMP for lending or borrowing assets as the native governance token behind the leading lending protocol. On the Compound Governance Dashboard, COMP governs important protocol decisions that can be voted on or delegated.

COMP is allocated to markets in proportion to the interest earned, which means that assets that earn the most interest make the most COMP per day. Here's an excellent tool for tracking which purchases earn the most COMP on any day.

Defi Rate is making a solid push to become a Compound delegate, and you can read about why you should consider delegating to us here.

Kyber Network – KNC

Total Supply: 210,623,056 KNC

Kyber Network is a leading DEX that captures value via a native token called Kyber Network Crystals (KNC). Fees from the exchange are primarily used to burn KNC. Kyber recently upgraded its Katalyst tokenomics, introducing fundamental governance mechanisms with the introduction of the KyberDAO.

Users will vote (or delegate) on important protocol decisions, such as distributing fees collected from DEX trading using KNC.

MKR stands for Maker.

The total supply is 1,005,577 MKR.

Maker is the decentralized lending protocol that gave rise to DAI. MKR is burned using a portion of Stability Fees collected from outstanding loans and is used to vote on protocol decisions via the Maker voting dashboard. Kyber Network is a leading DEX that captures value via a native token called Kyber Network Crystals (KNC). Fees from the exchange are primarily used to burn KNC. Kyber recently upgraded its Katalyst tokenomics, introducing fundamental governance mechanisms with the introduction of the KyberDAO.

Users will vote (or delegate) on important protocol decisions, such as distributing fees collected from DEX trading using KNC.

BAL stands for Balancer.

100,000,000 BAL is the total supply.

The balancer is a technology for automated asset management and liquidity governed by a native token called BAL. The balancer has seen rapid growth on all fronts since launching its Liquidity Mining program in June. BAL is utilized to govern critical protocol decisions such as protocol fees, support assets, and Factors about how BAL is earned.

UMA –

The total supply is 100,224,817 UMA.

UMA is a derivatives protocol used to generate permissionless synthetic assets.

The native token – UMA – governs protocol decisions and can challenge underlying registries that are out of sync with the synthetic asset they are attached to.

Curve – CRV

Total Supply of Curve – CRV: 3,030,000,000 CRV

The curve is a liquidity aggregator for assets with the same peg, such as stablecoins and Bitcoin wraps. The native token, CRV, is staked through the Curve DAO for time-weighted governance rights and liquidity multipliers on CRV liquidity mining. It has been suggested that the Curve DAO will employ protocol fees to purchase and burn CRV on the open market in the future.

ALPHA FINANCE – ALPHA FINANCE

1,000,000,000 total supply ALPHA

Alpha Finance is the yield farming aggregator behind Alpha Honora, which lends idle ETH to farm on leverage. ALPHA governs the risk-averse platform, with a portion of the yield directed back to a community treasury maintained by governance.

INDEX - Index Cooperative

INDEX TOTAL SUPPLY: 10,000,000

Index Cooperative is the index management protocol used by the Defi Pulse Index's community governance

(DPI). The INDEX governance token is used to determine how indexes are constructed and how the assets included inside those indexes are used in the meta-governance of their respective protocols. The same team runs the Index Co-op as Set Protocol and Token Sets.

Ren Protocol – REN

Total Supply of REN: 1,000,000,000

Ren Protocol is an interoperable bridge that allows assets to be transferred to Ethereum using the RenVM. Users must post 100,000 REN as collateral to run a dark node on the network to become a validator. Those who run a dark node are entitled to a pro-rata portion of all trading fees earned through the Protocol.

Nexus Mutual – NXM

Total Supply: 4,355,684 NXM

Nexus Mutual distributes NXM to mutual members in exchange for ETH placed in the Capital Pool to defend against smart contract vulnerabilities. ETH from the capital pool can reimburse the impacted party if a claim is approved. Members can stake NXM on various contracts to receive a percentage of the fees when covers are acquired. Nexus will soon implement pooled staking, allowing all surfaces purchased to be distributed among all people who stake their NXM.

Bancor – BNT

Total Supply: 69,148,554 BNT

Bancor is a decentralized exchange powered by a native cryptocurrency called BNT. A percentage of the exchange's trading fees are allocated to BNT holders. Bancor is launching a V2 upgrade that introduces BNT staking through a BancorDAO.

Loopring – LRC

Total Supply: 1,374,513,897 LRC

Loopring is a Layer 2 exchange protocol that provides scalability options to optimize Ethereum throughput. LRC is staked to earn a percentage of trading fees generated on the DEX and applications such as Loopring Pay.

Please keep in mind that this list will be updated regularly as new tokens come to our attention. If you would like to see your ticket on this list, please contact us to describe what your receipt is used for and why it should be included.

Numerai – NMR

Total Supply: 10,979,551 NMR

Numerai is an AI-powered hedge fund that developed Erasure, a prediction protocol in which users stake NMR to indicate their confidence in their predictions. NMR was recently added to the Coinbase platform.

bZx – BZRX

Total Supply: 1,030,000,000 BZRX

Loopring is a Layer 2 exchange protocol that provides scalability options to optimize Ethereum throughput.

LRC is staked to earn a percentage of trading fees generated on the DEX and applications such as Loopring Pay.

Please remember that this list will be updated regularly as new tokens come to our attention. Also, if you want your receipt to be included on this list, please get in touch with us to describe what it is used for and why it should be included.

PieDAO – DOUGH

Total Supply: 100,000,000 DOUGH

PieDAO is an automated asset management protocol that provides several Defi indexes. Its native token, DOUGH, manage the indexes and pays fees to DOUGH holders when the indexes are exchanged. DOUGH is now available through a variety of liquidity mining initiatives.

MTA Total Supply

Total supply: 100,000,000 MTA mStable

Mutable is a liquidity aggregator for tokens that share a peg, often called assets, such as required characteristics. The Protocol is managed by a native token, MTA, which can be staked via the Earn function to claim protocol fees and MTA inflation. MTA launched an Initial DEX Offering but chose Mesa for fair price discovery to minimize bot front-running. Loopring is a Layer 2 exchange protocol that offers scalability options to improve Ethereum throughput. LRC is staked to earn a share of trading fees made on the DEX and applications such as Loopring Pay.

CLOSING THOUGHTS

The Defi movement promises many benefits for customers and investors, including eliminating intermediaries and central oversight, increased retail investor access to financial markets, and new investment opportunities. To achieve their lofty goals, Defi developers are leveraging some fundamental properties of blockchain technology.

"Decentralized finance" already implies the Defi movement's distinguishing feature. That is unsurprising. Blockchain's value proposition is based on decentralization. The goal is to move away from relying on corporations and other institutions for oversight, server space, data storage, and so on. This is accomplished by ensuring that all blockchain network members have access to the same transaction history.

DAO

Origin of DAOs

A common mistake is to think that DAOs were born with Ethereum. While it is true that Ethereum brought this concept to much of the public in the Blockchain sector, the birth of DAOs came much earlier.

This innovative concept was initially postulated by Dilger de Werner, a renowned professor of computer science from Germany. It was Dilger who, in 1997, developed his work "Decentralized autonomous organization of the smart home based on the immune system principle" Dilger established the DAO's roots as a self-sustaining and autonomous system in it a work that was unquestionably ahead of its time. His plan, however, was unfeasible at the time. Until the emergence of blockchain, the technical hurdle of building a DAO could not be addressed.

It was then that the DAO idea came to the fore again. On September 7, 2013, Daniel Larimer, creator of BitShares y steem, would talk about them on Let's Talk Bitcoin! Until then, Daniel spoke of them as Decentralized Autonomous Companies (CAD), another common way of calling DAOs. It was not until 2015 when Vitalik Buterin would relaunch the concept thanks to the launch of Ethereum, which allowed to creation of advanced transparent and immutable (full Turing) code, something that made creating and interacting with DAOs much easier.

WHAT IS DAO?

The Decentralized Autonomous Organization (DAO) is a system without central management. Decisions are made from the ground up, managed by a community organized to implement a specific set of rules in the blockchain. DAOs are Internet organizations that are collectively owned and managed by their members. They come with built-in coffers that can just be obtained with the authorization of the members. Decisions are made by the exhortation that the group votes on over a set period of time.

A decentralized autonomous organization (DAO) can accomplish a range of goals without the requirement for hierarchical supervision. These organizations can form freelancer networks, philanthropic organizations, and venture capital firms that pool their cash to pay for software subscriptions, as well as philanthropic organizations where members approve payments.

The core constituents of a DAO

It's important to note that the underlying processes of DAOs can differ between blockchain initiatives. However, any DAO must go through three critical stages in order to be successfully launched. Smart contract integration, token creation, and deployment are three of them. Smart contracts, on the other hand, are the cornerstone of all DAOs, therefore ensuring their smooth and proper implementation is critical.

Smart contract integration to begin, a DAO's rules must be defined and encoded in a series of smart contracts.

Setting up smart contracts carefully is critical to developing a long-term and flexible DAO. Otherwise, faults committed at the start of the project can derail it completely.

⬦ Token creation

Smart contracts aren't the only thing that a DAO needs to work properly. The development of native tokens must also be taken into account.

When creating smart contracts, make sure they allow for the generation and distribution of native tokens, which will be used in voting processes and to incentivize specific DAO actions.

It's worth noting that there are numerous things that can be voted on in a DAO, the most frequent of which are:

- ✓ Expenditures are made or planned by the organization
- ✓ Product choices that will be on the Dao roadmap
- ✓ different Upgrade protocols and new technology implementation
- ✓ Members/contributors which can be added to the network
- ✓ How potential profit will be shared among all DAO members and contracted agents.

✛ DAO deployment

A sufficient budget is required for the deployment of a DAO. If this condition is met, all DAO members' proposed decisions will be decided by a consensus vote. As a result, all token holders are automatically turned into stakeholders with the ability to make ideas about the DAO's future work and how its assets should be distributed.

A well-defined token distribution policy and consensus mechanism should be included in the smart contract architecture. As a result, the DAO's participants will have all of the conditions in place for the network's effective development.

DAOs in all shapes and sizes

According to Decrypt, DAOs can have different configurations, depending on the purpose of each one:

1. **Crypto projects:** Crypto projects that are managed by decentralized governance, in which token holders vote on the direction of the project, can be considered as DAOs. An example of this category of DAO is MakerDAO.

111

Financing: An autonomous decentralized organization can also be used to provide development funds, depending on established criteria. An example of this type of DAO is MolochDAO.

2. **Investments:** some for-profit DAOs were generated from forks of other organizations, as happened with MolochDAO. In this category of decentralized autonomous organization, shares, and other assets are distributed among community members, as is the case with MetaCartel Ventures.

3. **Collection:** Non-fungible tokens (NFTs) became a fever during the year 2021. With that, some DAOs emerged focused on raising funds for the acquisition of these tokens, as FlamingoDAO does. In this type of organization, members can share the rights to the NFTs, in addition to lending them or exhibiting them in some digital art gallery. The community will decide what will be done with the NFTs it acquires.

Key characteristics of a DAO

The rules for DAO are encoded in clever ideological contracts. And from there, any DAO member can propose changes. However, the weight of the proposal in good faith for the right to vote is determined by the number of management members the member holds, which plays an important role in gaining a better place at the table.

Here are some of the key attributes of DAO that set it apart from any traditional organ.

- ✓ A group of core people comes with the concept.
- ✓ Fully visible framework
- ✓ There is no one in charge, and it can be verified at various points.
- ✓ Any Dao member can see the financial aspects of the company without difficulty, making it publicly audited.
- ✓ Changes in the code or protocol must be selected transparently.
- ✓ Defi, NFT, and cases of utilitarian use can all be built into the system.

Types of DAO & the relevant Blockchain

Depending on its organization, modus operandi, and technology, a DAO can fall into one of the following categories:

1. **Operating Systems–** Standalone platforms that allow organizations to create their own DAOs. Key projects include Orca and Colony.

2. **Protocol DAOs–** Protocol DAOs are decentralized autonomous organizations that perform protocol and financial modifications using tokens as a voting metric. Uniswap, Maker, Yearn, Synthetic, Curve, and other projects are among the most important.

3. **Investment DAOs–** Allows funds to be pooled for a variety of Defi operations and investments. The LAO, BitDAO, and other important projects are among them.

4. **Grants DAOs** — Similar to decentralized Venture Capitalists with communities, where governance tokens are used to vote on fund

allocation. Audius Grants, MolochDAO, and other important projects are among them.

5. **Collector DAOs–** Meant for NFTs and artists to support fractional or complete ownership of art and content. Key projects include Flamingo.

6. **Service DAOs–** Talent hunting and acquisition model for agencies and individuals. Key projects include MetaverseDAO, DaoHaus, and more.

7. **Social DAOs–** A decentralized platform for social networking interactions. Seed Club, FWB, and other important projects are among them.

8. **Media DAOs–** More akin to a decentralized news aggregator that is transparent and serves the common good of its users. The mirror is one of the most important projects.

Investors should pay special attention to the tokens associated with these DAOs, as they will influence their position and decision-making authority in the ecosystem.

How does a DAO work?

As mentioned earlier, the DAO is an organization where a group of members makes decisions from the beginning. DAO can be involved in several ways, the most popular of which is holding a token.

DAOs made use of smart contracts, which are essentially bits of code that run automatically when a set of criteria is met. Smart contracts are now employed on a variety of blockchains, including Ethereum, which was the first. These smart contracts establish the DAO's regulations. DAOs made use of smart contracts, which are essentially bits of code that run automatically when a set of criteria is met. Smart contracts are now employed on a variety of blockchains, including Ethereum, which was the first. These smart contracts establish the DAO's regulations. This model blocks the advice from being sent to Daos: only when most stakeholders agree to the plan will it become law—the method for determining that the majority varies from Dao to Dao and is described in a smart contract.

Dao is fully independent and transparent. Anyone can see their code because they are built on Open-Source blockchains. Because Blockchain records all financial transactions, anyone can audit their default treasury.

Steps For Launching Dao

⊹ Smart contract creation

First, the developer or group of developers must create a smart DAO contract. At startup, they can change the rules in these contracts only through the management system. This means that they have to test contracts to make sure they don't forget important details.

⊹ Funding

After concluding smart contracts, the DAO must determine how to obtain funding and how you can administer it. More often, tokens are sold to raise funds; these tokens give holders the right to vote.

⊹ Deployment

Once everything is set up, DAO must be deployed in a blockchain. From this moment on, stakeholders decide on the future of the organization. The creators of the organization - those who write smart contracts - cannot influence the project any more than other stakeholders.

Why do we need DAOs?

As a nationwide organization on the Internet, DAOs have many advantages over traditional organizations. The main advantage of DAO is the lack of trust between the two parties. While a traditional organization needs a lot of trust from the people behind it - especially investors - with a DAO, the code simply needs to be reliable. This code is easier to rely on because it is publicly available and can be extensively tested before it runs. Every action taken by the DAO after launch must be approved by the community and must be completely transparent and controllable.

In such an organization, there is no hierarchy. Despite this, it can fulfill tasks and grow while under the control of its native token. Because there is no hierarchy, any collaborator can present an original idea that the entire group will consider and enhance. Internal issues are typically settled swiftly by voting, which adheres to the smart contract's pre-written laws. DAOs enable investors to pool funds and invest in early-stage startups and decentralized projects while sharing the risk and potential profits.

The principal-agent dilemma

The main advantage of Dao is that they offer solutions for the main agent dilemma. This dilemma is a conflict in the priority between a person or group (principal) and those who make decisions and act on their behalf (agent).

Problems can occur in several situations, with those that are common in the relationship between stakeholders and CEOs. Agents (CEOs) can work in a way that is not in line with the priorities and objectives determined by the principal (stakeholders) and instead of acting based on their own personal interests.

Another typical example of the main agent dilemma occurs when agents take the excessive risk because the principal bears the burden. For example, a trader can use extreme leverage to pursue a bonus performance, knowing the organization will include a downside.

Dao solves the main agent dilemma through community governance. Stakeholders are not forced to join Dao and only do it after understanding the rules that regulate it. They don't need to trust any agents that act on their behalf instead of working as part of the group whose incentives are in harmony. The interests of token holders parallel to the nature of Dao encourage them to harmlessly. Because they have shared it on the network, they will want to see it succeed. Acting against it will act against their self-interest.

Dao's advantages and disadvantages

Like all types of technology, Dao can offer superiority and different losses. Something very true because they depend on the schedule or regulation of Dao. However, at this point, we can generalize some well-known points.

Benefits

Allows you to create organizations without any hierarchy. Decentralizing the organization allows everyone who is a part of it to contribute ideas and vote on them.

It has a high level of transparency. This is because a DAO inherits from blockchain technology the capacity to record and publish all acts having taken, as well as access the source code of its operations.

Decentralization enables DAOs to provide services worldwide, removing borders and democratizing access to services that would otherwise be unavailable to the general public.

They make it much easier to create organizations as they have to be programmed only on a blockchain, and from that moment, they start to work. This saves money, time, and paperwork, which is necessary for a traditional organization or business registration.

Disadvantages

It is not simple to program a DAO. The capacity to automate operations and make decisions is extremely difficult. A single line error can result in millions of euros in losses, as the DAO case demonstrated.

There are issues with DAOs complying with regulations in many countries. This is good because blockchain technology and cryptocurrencies do not yet have clear regulations.

Just a few years after their creation, DAOs are undoubtedly an incredible technological tool that can be part of any main revolution in the future. Certainly, this revolution ends up coming from people not conditioned by the current limitations of society, visionaries. Who knows, maybe that person is you.

Ethereum and "The DAO"

One of the earliest examples of DAO was aptly named "The DAO." It was made up of composite smart contracts running on top of the Ethereum blockchain, which was supposed to behave as an autonomous venture fund.

The DAO tokens, which gave an equity share and voting rights in this decentralized fund, were sold in an Initial Coin Offering (ICO). However, shortly after its launch, about a third of its funds were withdrawn in one of the most numerous hacker attacks in the history of cryptocurrencies.

The result of this affair was that Ethereum split into two chains after a hard fork. In one, fraudulent transactions were effectively rolled back as if the hack had never happened. This chain is now called the Ethereum blockchain. The other chain, respecting the "code is law" principle, left fraudulent transactions untouched and maintained immutability. This blockchain is now called Ethereum Classic.

Overview of a few of the most popular DAOs

Supply chain, data and asset administration, healthcare, and the Internet of Things are just a few of the industries where decentralized autonomous organizations have been successfully deployed (IoT). DAOs, on the other hand, are particularly significant to the Defi field. They can be used in some Defi use cases, such as crypto lending and yield farming, to let crypto traders carry out trades with cryptocurrencies. Despite the failure of the original DAO project (The DAO), it did not prevent the creation and development of subsequent DAOs, which provide several advantages over existing alternatives.

The entire DAO ecosystem currently includes a multitude of DAO platforms and is eager to welcome new members into its ranks. PixelPlex's team of professional software developers took a break and brought out an abacus to count how many DAOs had been created so far. Sure enough, we'd lost track. But keep your chin up! We chose the most well-known DAO platforms and DSaaS (DAO Software-as-a-Service) vendors to showcase. Take a look at them!

↓ DAOstack

DAOstack is an open-source DAO platform that allows developers to create decentralized apps (dApps), DAOs, and a variety of DAO tools. It comes with a modular smart contract framework, a javascript developer environment, and a user-friendly interface that allows anyone to start and/or join a decentralized organization.

DAOstack was created with the goal of supporting a global collaborative network and assisting in the formation of organizations for any type of collaborative work, such as:

- ✓ Asset administration (venture, pension, and charitable funds, insurance networks)

- ✓ Asset management (venture, pensions and charity funds, insurance networks)
- ✓ Curation network (restaurant and hotel guides, website listings, articles, and video feeds)

GEN, DAOstack's native token, is also available. It gives platform users a core utility within decentralized organizations and enables them to scale efficiently. Prime DAO, necDAO, dOrg, DXdao, and Genesis Alpha are some of the most well-known decentralized autonomous organizations built on DAOstack.

⊥ Aragon

Aragon is a set of tools and services for forming and managing decentralized autonomous groups based on the Ethereum blockchain and the Rinkeby network.

Aragon's software can be used to create clubs, NGOs, and other groups that use its decentralized system to manage finances and make decisions collaboratively. Another advantage of Aragon is that it is very scalable, allowing users to create a wide range of complex features. More than 1,700 organizations have been formed on Aragon so far, according to the Aragon community. The platform has also been utilized to generate enterprises like Curve, Decentraland, and Pool Together, which have a combined market worth of almost $3 billion.

The Aragon Client (a specific tool for forming and participating in DAOs), the Aragon Network (a DAO made up of a wide network of DAOs), the Aragon Association (a nonprofit organization responsible for dispersing Aragon token sales revenues), and Aragon Court make up Aragon (a system for resolving disputes). Aragon also includes two native tokens, ANT and ANJ, which are utilized in the administration of the Aragon Network DAO and the debate resolution mechanism.

⊹ MakerDAO

Maker Dao is generally regarded as one of the largest decentralized autonomous organizations. It operates as an autonomous-based loan platform based on Ethereum and DAI coin providers. Maker Dao uses the DAO structure for governance decisions and to support operations in all decentralized loan systems. And this, the makerdao is related to developing technology for loans and savings. It has also erected a special protocol that allows anyone with ETH and metamask wallets to lend Dai Stablecoins. When the user locks several ETH in the Smart Makerdao contract, they are able to produce certain DAI counts: the more et al. one, the more dai will be produced.

Aside from DAI, there is also maker (MKR), which was made by Makermao with the aim of providing stability to the Token Dai Makerdao and allowing the right management in the DAI credit system.

Maker Dao is generally referred to as one of the leading projects of the DEFI movement because of several high-profile partnerships that contribute to wider adoption.

Moloch Dao.

Moloch Dao has gained many advantages because of his main initiative to help fund the development of Ethereum 2.0. This Dao depends on relatively simple smart contract functionality that helps reduce the number of potential attacks. It should also be noted that this intelligent contract has branched out to launch many other DAO, including Metacartel Ventures and Marketing Dao.

Moloch Dao also provides grants for those who contribute to further progress from the Ethereum ecosystem. Another strange feature of this Dao is the mechanism of "anger" is innate. This means that a member of Molych can be literally angry to stop and pull their tokens if they do not agree with certain community decisions.

Since its launch, Moloch Dao has control to collect more than $ 1 million in contributions from several largest Ethereum companies and even Group members.

⊹ Colony

The colony is a protocol that helps create autonomous organizations decentralized through Open Source, Ethereum-based smart contracts. It also offers its users a common purpose framework that helps in carrying out key functions that sometimes cannot be managed by organizations, including handling ownership and authority and financial management.

Colony networks allow the formation of autonomous organizations to be decentralized supply them with the necessary infrastructure. It also allows participants to manage their funds effectively with the help of strong on-chain governance and decision-making mechanisms.

The colony network has an original Clny utility token that provides the following rights to holders:

- ✓ The right to grip part in the process of mining network internal reputation
- ✓ The right to join the network management process
- ✓ The right to claim part of net income

Overall, Colony is a highly efficient and high-performance platform designed for community collaboration. This simplifies the decision-making and financial management process.

Wrap

Despite the reality that the first Dao fell, this did not stop the initiation and spread of hundreds of other Dao projects. The core principle of decentralization has triggered interest in various industries and has proven to be a real driving force behind innovation and increased efficiency.

Decentralized autonomous organizations are believed to play an important role in our future society, bringing better and fairer management with greater transparency. Through the wisdom of the crowd, it is possible to make rapid collective decisions and improve organizational functions.

If you want to made your own strong Dao from the beginning, then you will be advised to delegate the task to the DAPP Developer team experts with the Knack to produce top-notch solutions. They will ensure development, deployment, and support that are smooth and can also build sophisticated DLT ecosystems around it.

A decentralized future is just around the corner. Start shifting to the new rail now and is in the right place when it arrives.

How to buy DAO Invest

Some cryptocurrencies, like DAO Invest, can only be purchased with another cryptocurrency on decentralized exchanges. To buy DAO Invest, you'll need to first purchase Ethereum (ETH) and then use ETH to buy DAO Invest. And for that, you need a so-called self-custody wallet. Here is how to do it with Coinbase Wallet for US residents.

1. Download Coinbase Wallet

A self-custody wallet like Coinbase Wallet is needed to buy DAO Invest. Coinbase Wallet is reachable as a mobile app and browser extension.

2. Choose a Coinbase Wallet username

You will need to select a username when setting up your Coinbase Wallet. This username allows other Coinbase Wallet users to easily send you cryptocurrencies. You can keep your username exclusive, but you need them to access your account.

3. Securely store your recovery phrase

When you create your own new wallet, you will receive a collection set consisting of 12 random words. The word recovery is the key to your cryptocurrency, which means that everyone with your recovery kit has access to your cryptocurrency. Do not share your word of healing with anyone. We advocate that you write it down and keep it safe, as well as use the Coinbase Wallet cloud backup feature.

Remember not to share your word of healing with anyone. Coinbase will never request your recovery phrase. And if you lose your recovery kit, Coinbase will not be able to help you retrieve your wallet.

4. Recognize and budget for Ethereum network fees.

Fees differ depending on how busy the network is, how complicated the transaction is, and how quickly you want the transaction to complete—plan to deposit money into accounts.

5. Buy et and deposit it to your coin wallet.

If you do not have a Coinbas account, you will need to create one to purchase Ethereum (ETH). Learn more about creating a Coinbase account and purchasing Ethereum (ETH). How you transfer ETH to Coinbase Wallet will vary depending on whether you use the mobile app or the Chrome extension.

6. Use your ETH to buy DAO Invest in the trade tab

If you use a coinbase wallet on your mobile, you can buy DAO to invest right in the application. Tap the CoinBase wallet application image. Then valve on the "Trade" tab, where you can exchange ETH for any tokens that run on the Ethereum standard (called "Erc-

20 tokens"). Tap "Choose Coins" and select Dao Invest. Enter the number of et which you want to exchange to invest in Dao. Remember to leave enough transaction fees. Confirm your purchase and follow the order on the screen to complete.

If you use a coinbase wallet extension, tap the "Conversion" button. Find Dao Invest and enter the number of et which you want to exchange to invest in Dao. Remember to leave enough transaction fees. Certify your purchase and follow the instructions on the screen to complete.

What are the main challenges encountered by this technology?

This ease and cost reduction in negotiations can suffer from some challenges. Among them, we can mention:

✦ Legality

The legal scope can be one of the barriers faced by an Autonomous Decentralized Organization. This happens because a company is recognized through a legal entity, according to the legislation in force in Brazil.

However, one of the major points of the new autonomous organizations is precisely decentralization; that is, there is no representative — a legal entity — to be responsible for their structures.

⊹ Safety

Fortunately, the code of a DAO is visible to all users, and if there is a flaw, the security of that code can be considered a threat by malicious members, causing damage to the project. This security (or lack thereof) is influenced by the platform used for trading.

As happened recently, when several bugs were found in various tokens on the Ethereum network.

⊹ Decision Process

There is no team or representative responsible for studying and considering proposals. Therefore, the considerations and criteria for evaluating a project are left to the members of the organizations.

With this, decisions must be an agreement between all members, as the non-consent of just one is enough for the autonomous organization to consider this divergent opinion. Therefore, agreement and responsibility are required in any decision-making that affects the progress of the vote and the project itself.

The Decentralized Autonomous Organization allows for ease, speed, cost savings, and transparency in its processes. However, as it is still a recent technology on the market, it may leave some points to be desired.

Future of a DAO

DAOs are the Next Step

Smart contracts are very beneficial for automating transactional operations and decreasing the amount of data that humans have to provide for relatively simple jobs. A Decentralized Autonomous Organization's goal isn't only to limit human inputs; it's to completely eradicate them. A DAO is essentially a corporation that employs an interconnected web of smart contracts to automate all of its critical and non-essential procedures; however, it is still mostly an on-paper idea rather than one that has been refined in practice.

A model with DAO-like aims can help any company. A novelty keychain business with ledger-based inventory can develop a smart contract that triggers each item's unique reorder point based on previous client demand. The smart contract will generate, submit, and specify the delivery date for an invoice for the store's relevant supplier. When the package comes, the smart contract will be notified through scanners or IoT beacons connected to the blockchain and will release a cryptocurrency payout. When orders come in, it can gather client information from a CRM system, print labels automatically, and help expedite shipping.

Companies that use DAO platforms to divide and automate certain aspects of their business can achieve rapid scalability and become more robust without sacrificing quality. However, there are some obstacles that make it difficult to achieve real DAO at the moment. Access to technologies such as IoT beacons is still limited, which means that an organization that deals with physical products always need human labor until robots are cheaper and easier to use. In addition, the idea of a self-management system requires an additional level of complexity with each passing day. Doing business has never been easier, so good DAO has much more to consider when it comes to smooth and honest operations. Starting faster artificial intelligence could also be unexpected for DAO. While organizations that are about to be considered DAOs still require users to vote on protocol changes, for example, AI-based DAOs are one day programmed to autonomously consider the preferences of millions of individual stakeholders simultaneously. While DAOs are still years away from full autonomy, smart companies can now identify areas where inputs are excessive before using the DAO technology component to streamline operations without worrying that their lives will be destroyed.

Dangers and Risks in DAO

DAOs, according to experts, still have a long way to go because of their novelty and ties to a male-dominated web3 environment, despite the fact that their Discord discussions are open to practically everyone.

While DAOs promise transparency and ownership, it's difficult to call them democratic because people who can't buy larger stakes have less influence over group decisions. DAOs, like other new web3 technologies, allow for massive capital transfers with no oversight or formal control. Those lured to DAOs' notion of the community may nonetheless be concerned about losing their money or being victims of fraud.

Given the current regulatory gray area in which they operate, joining a DAO can be risky. DAOs are not subject to a particular legal structure in most U.S. states; therefore, protocol developers and participants face greater liability than stockholders of regulated organizations.

What is the legal status of DAOs?

While DAOs are strikingly similar to conventional businesses, only a few jurisdictions throughout the world recognize them as legal entities entitled to the same protections as traditional businesses like LLCs. Wyoming, in the United States, is one of these jurisdictions, having approved laws in April allowing DAOs to register as finite liability companies (LLCs). DAOs are also recognized as viable legal entities in Malta, a European country.

While there is considerable interest in recognizing DAOs as new legal organizations, most DAOs operate under ordinary partnership laws, which may subject DAO members to any obligations or liabilities incurred by the DAO. To address this problem, projects such as Open Law have sprung up, promising a liability wrapper for DAOs that will allow them to operate safely. Despite this, the majority of DAOs continue to function without any traditional liability protection for their members.

www.ingramcontent.com/pod-product-compliance
Lightning Source LLC
Chambersburg PA
CBHW032004190326
41520CB00007B/357